Deal Structure

OVERTIME

The Good, The Bad, and The Ugly Exposed

by CHRIS PREFONTAINE

with ZACHARY BEACH & NICK PREFONTAINE

featuring BRIAN O'NEILL, RUSSELL HAM, GREG & CAMI GOUCHER and CHAD HEETER

The Best-Selling Authors of **Real Estate On Your Terms** and **The New Rules Of Real Estate Investing**

WWW.SMARTREALESTATECOACH.COM

Written by Chris Prefontaine, Zachary Beach, and Nick Prefontaine
with Brian O'Neill, Russell Ham, Cami & Greg Goucher, and Chad Heeter
Edited by Ryan Staples

Requests for permission should be made to:
support@smartrealestatecoach.com

Published by Wicked Smart Books
www.WickedSmartBooks.com

ISBN: 978-0-578-95412-7

Printed in The United States of America

This publication is designed to provide accurate and authoritative information in regard to the subject matter covered. It is sold with the understanding that the publisher is not engaged in rendering legal, accounting, or other professional services. If legal advice or other expert assistance is required, the services of a competent professional person should be sought.

TABLE OF CONTENTS //

INTRODUCTION

BASIC DEALS

ADVANCED DEALS

SUMMARY

WHAT CAN GO WRONG? //
THE GOOD, THE BAD, AND THE UGLY EXPOSED

Most courses and events out there (no need to mention any names or throw anyone under the bus) paint a nice rosy picture, so as to not "scare" you from not entering the business model they teach. Yes, that was an exact statement from another educator who I know. Relative to my chapter in our best-selling book *Real Estate On Your Terms,* he said, *"Why are you doing that? You'll scare people away from doing real estate – don't share that much detail."*

See, I feel the complete opposite. I want you to be equipped to handle reality. I want you to go into a deal *expecting* curve balls and then understand how to properly pivot and not only handle them but profit even more from them. We teach our unique 3 Paydays™ system, as well as how to eke out a 4th and 5th Payday; sometimes those come from the curve balls, the challenges in the deals. Welcome them... once we show you how to handle them and once you have us on your team!

I really do wish it was as easy as some of the educators will lead you to believe and I really do wish you could just take a course or attend an event and become a real estate millionaire overnight like they suggest. Fortunately, we've set up our Genius Model to help you nail all areas of the business that we know for certain are necessary and it doesn't stop with understanding deals. However, understanding how to structure deals creatively is a huge part of the skillset pillar in our Genius Model. If you go through the hundreds of deals that we have on YouTube (you'll want to subscribe, so you don't miss any) you'll notice that not one deal is the same. Inside of the three different ways we buy – lease purchase, owner financing and sub-to – there are so many nuances and different ways to get to 3 Paydays™ and the more exposure to them the better and more profitable you and your deals will be.

Getting the knowledge that is contained in our Genius Model is not enough because *execution trumps knowledge* every day of the week. How do we get ourselves to execute? How do we get ourselves to take action? Well, for starters, just hang out with us and the Wicked Smart Community. Your constant exposure to deal structures and to us will put you into action, which starts to create results, which builds your confidence, certainty, and belief which then up levels your potential and the cycle continues. We're here to help you create the life of your dreams.

Think HUGE!

Chris Prefontaine

WHAT IS DEAL STRUCTURE OVERTIME? //

In early 2018, we started a weekly series on our *Smart Real Estate Coach* YouTube channel called **Deal Structure Sundays**. At the time of this writing, for the past 160 weeks, a video has been published each-and-every Sunday since then that focuses on the intricacies of this business. Sometimes the video includes an interview with an Associate from our *Wicked Smart Community* about a property that they just got under contract. Other times, the video focuses on a specific part of our niche that need a flashlight shone on it. Regardless of the length or the specific content, the goal is to help aspiring real estate investors understand a bit more of the terms niche that might be difficult without some real-world examples.

Fast-forward to the Fall of 2020, we found that the 8-to-10-minute clips released each week weren't quite long enough to contain all of the nuances in these deals. As the world got more complicated, so did our transactions. Terms got lengthier, new-and-exciting pivots were introduced, life events happened, buyers walked away from properties; the truth is, how could we be expected to give our viewers the stories of these deals, blemishes-and-all, as we were watching the clock. So, as a part of our *Smart Real Estate Coach Academy*, we rolled out a new course called **Deal Structure Overtime**.

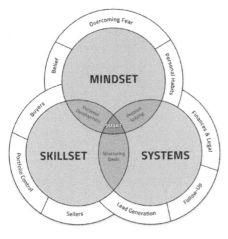

The reason that we did this is because of what we call our **Genius Model**. It's broken down into three parts: Mindset, Skillset, and Systems. Our theory is that if an Associate can master all three of those areas, that's what will truly make them a *Wicked Smart* Investor. Well, it's probably no surprise that the Deal Structure Overtime videos include elements of all 3 facets of this model.

Now, each time we release an interview with an Associate, we do so in two parts. The first part goes out for free, as it always has, over social media. These clips go through all 3 Paydays™ and give a 10,000-foot view of how the deal was structured and what the Associate can expect to profit from them. The second part of the video interview is loaded into the Deal Structure Overtime course that is shared with members of our *Wicked Smart Community* and lives in our self-guided online academy at www.SmartRealEstateCoachAcademy.com. Those clips are chock full of all the nuts-and-bolts, true-to-life stories that make up the day-to-day of our investment business.

This book is a taste of what those videos are like. We have transcripts from 8 different deals, edited only for fluidity and readability, that highlight some basic deals and some more advanced deals. So, dive in, pore over the numbers, and then try your hand at starting your own real estate investment business. We'd be more than happy to talk about what that might look like for you if you schedule a FREE strategy call. Just visit www.smartrealestatecoach.com/action and make your appointment today.

Enjoy the book!

GET YOUR MINDSET STRAIGHT //

On this Deal Structure Sunday, Chris calls up Chad Heeter, a High 6 Associate from Colorado. In this chapter, they discuss the importance of mindset, how to approach a conversation with a seller that already has an agent, and the value of a deal's term extension.

Chris Prefontaine:	When you get your mindset straight, you get your deal flow straight. Chad, I couldn't wait to get you on here and do this. I want to hit the mindset stuff, but first I want to talk about this deal that we just got done.
Chad Heeter:	Yeah. Of course.
Chris Prefontaine:	The source of this was what?
Chad Heeter:	It was an expired Slybroadcast from about 6 months ago, actually.
Chris Prefontaine:	How many did you send out with that broadcast? What's typical?
Chad Heeter:	It's typically around 350.
Chris Prefontaine:	So, 350 people get a message on their voicemail from Chad. And then we have a series of automated messages to follow that – but this was a call back from June or you were following up and it came up?
Chad Heeter:	It was a callback from June; I had a good chat with the seller. He was a retired Navy officer. He built this beautiful... I wouldn't call it a cabinet. It's a typical log

home for Colorado. Hand-scraped, local lumber, truly a gorgeous home. He told me it was the last place that he was expecting to buy and live in and retire in. He built it about 7 or 8 years ago.

Not long after, he met someone and they moved back to South Carolina. They would come out to this house for a couple months a year, but in the last couple of years he decided to sell it. He had it on the market with a real estate agent for a year, it expired, and then we talked. I went out to see the property, took photos, we went back and forth on some numbers, and the next day I saw that it was listed with another real estate agent.

Chris Prefontaine: That happens a lot, just so I can interject that. For those reading this, we don't bum out. We go, "Okay, they'll be back if it doesn't sell." And most of them don't sell.

Chad Heeter: I left him a friendly message that said, "Hey, it looks like you're using another means of sale. If anything changes, just let me know."

Chris Prefontaine: On top of that, let me add a script for the readers. So, when it goes to another agent, don't bottom out. Say to the owner, "How long are you tied up for?" *Tied Up For* as the key phrase because real estate agents tie them up.

"Okay, great. Listen, if you don't get full price," another key phrase, "in the timeframe that you want or if you cancel, give me a call."

That's kind of how we position it.

Chad Heeter: Then, going through my leads that I do each day, I always go back and do follow up. I have things in the calendar to check on. Past leads. I'll see where they are, I'll text them, I'll email them, I might look up the property and see if it's sold. If it hasn't, which was the case with this guy, I left a message and said, "Hey, looks like your home still on market. If you want to have another conversation, give me a call." He called back that day said, "I put the house on the market with this agent and I haven't heard from them for three months."

Without much more salesmanship that that, he said, "Why not? Let's give it a shot."

Chris Prefontaine: Awesome. Let's talk numbers. He was listed for how much?

Chad Heeter: $499,000.

Chris Prefontaine: And how much does he owe?

Chad Heeter: He's free and clear.

Chris Prefontaine: Perfect, so we put it under agreement for how much?

Chad Heeter: $449,000 – because that was the number that his agent suggested that he drop it to.

Chris Prefontaine: This is great. This next part is so important for the readers. At $449,000, we structured what kind of monthly payments, Chad?

Chad Heeter:	$1,590.
Chris Prefontaine:	And what do you think you could get in the open market for that? Not counting taxes.
Chad Heeter:	$2,200.
Chris Prefontaine:	You're talking about 600 bucks per month as a spread. And then how long did we get the term on this one?
Chad Heeter:	36 months.
Chris Prefontaine:	This is shaping up to be a pretty cool deal here. What did we go on the market for?
Chad Heeter:	$499,000.
Chris Prefontaine:	Just what he was on for initially. So, this is not going to ruffle any feathers in the market. No one's going to say, "Oh, I would start lower." You can go down whenever you want – you can't go up later.
	Now, let's get to the interesting ingredients. We're talking to a buyer – and I just want these guys to know as a side note that because Chad's an associate, when you're in the newer stages of vetting buyers, just like when you're in the newer stages of vetting sellers, you can utilize our team.
Chad Heeter:	The next step forms were submitted and now the ball's in the buyer's court to see if he can come up a little bit on the deposit, which we both think he will.

Chris Prefontaine: Let's use him as the example because tomorrow someone else could walk in with a big juicy check. It happens. But let's use this guy for a conservative estimate on this deal. Where are we at for Payday #1?

Chad Heeter: Payday #1 would be $15,000 upfront, and then another $10,000 five months from now.

Chris Prefontaine: All with the outlook that you're going to get this deposit bigger than 25 grand, because he needs to be more financially committed to the property.

Chad Heeter: Correct.

Chris Prefontaine: The goal is always to get the buyer to at least 10% of the purchase price on this thing before they go get traditional financing. Ultimately, with this commitment to the property and keeping their credit up, that will get them a better rate. It's for your benefit as the investor and for their benefit in the long term.

Chad Heeter: And he understands that. He's self-employed, so he definitely understands that.

Chris Prefontaine: And needs time as someone who is self-employed, which is a key buyer for us, to build up his mortgage readiness.

Okay. Payday #2, how's it looking with that nice spread?

Chad Heeter: The spread is $610. Over 36 months, that's $21,960.

Chris Prefontaine:	That's a nice one. And then Payday #3?
Chad Heeter:	Well, if we're working on his down payment number of $25,000, the Payday #3 would be the price premium of $50,000, less his down payment, and then the principal paydown, which is $1,590 per month for a total of $57,240.
Chris Prefontaine:	Before you go on, that's huge for the readers to see. Just the principal pay down on a 36 month free and clear deal is almost 60 grand. That's huge. If you're ever able to extend this deal, which is something we do quite often, if maybe the buyer wants some more time, that could be an extra 5 figures on top of what we have here. We call these little plays Payday #4s.
	So, if you total the spread, the principal paydown and you minus the 25 they already gave you, what are we looking at?
Chad Heeter:	$82,240 for a total profit of $129,200.
Chris Prefontaine:	130 grand on a $449,000 purchase price, owner financing. That's pretty cool, guys.
Chad Heeter:	Yeah, it's a fantastic deal. And the seller was ecstatic too, as I was keeping in touch with him, because for 14 months he had maybe two showings with the two real estate agents. Then, within a few weeks, we had a couple showings and this current offer is on the table. So, when I talked with the seller the other day, he just assumed this thing wasn't going to sell for months. He

was beside himself, thinking, "Oh my gosh. Now I actually have to move my stuff."

Chris Prefontaine: But even when there's stress, it's a win-win-win.

DEAL TYPE:	Owner Financing	DEBT: $	0
SOURCE:	Slybroadcast Expired	EQUITY: $	449,000
TERM:	36 Months	SOLD: $	499,000

PAYDAY #1	
Deposit from Buyer	$ 15,000 + $10,000 = **$25,000**

PAYDAY #2	
Monthly Payment	$ 1,590
Payment From Buyer	$ 2,200
Monthly Cash Flow	$ 610 x 36 months = **$21,960**

PAYDAY #3	
Price Premium	$ 50,000
Principal Paydown	$ 1,590 x 36 months = **$57,240**
— Payday #1 Deposit	$ 25,000
Cash Out Payment	$ 82,240

TOTAL PROFIT: $ 129,200

Chad Heeter: Exactly. It's a win for the buyer as well. He has a home now where he wouldn't have been able to buy a house like this conventionally. That's the best part of the business.

Chris Prefontaine: Okay, so before we wrap up, why did I say at the beginning that, "when you get your head straight, you get your deal flow going"?

Chad Heeter: In building the kind of business that I want to build, and what most Associates want to build, it can be overwhelming. The numbers, the potential of it all. And if you're not used to making that level of income, to having access to this kind of money, you need to start working on a new mindset. Because there's just so many things that are going to creep in that are going to tell you, "It can't be done. It can't be done."

And so, through different suggestions that you've made, through speakers at our events, I've just taken those on. And it's been a daily thing, a weekly thing, monthly, just learning about how I can remove the roadblocks, clarify my thinking, and move into a new level of earning that I never had before.

So, that's a short answer. And I'll say that it hasn't been easy. I said the other day, learning the scripts is super important, learning how the business operates is super important, but there's a point in which you've got to work on yourself.

And I don't care who you are, what stage in life you might be at, there's always something you're going to need to be working on. So, those things just continue to be worked on. I've done all kinds of kinds of improvements in my life in the past year. Beyond building the business, it's mindset. It's physical stuff, meditation, all this stuff that's just been a lot of improvement in my life, that I've needed for both financial and personal reasons.

Chris Prefontaine: I love it. I couldn't have scripted that summary. It's important for these readers to know that when they become part of the Wicked Smart Community, these are the things that we talk about and we work on. None of this is going to pan out if you don't get your head straight. And why are we able to recognize that? Because we've gone through the same stuff. We all go through it, so we've got to keep working on it.

Chad Heeter: Yep. That's right.

HOW TO FIND THE PERFECT BUYER //

In this chapter, Chris chats with High 6 Associate and Strategy Expert, Brian O'Neill. Together, they cover finding the "perfect" buyer and how an expired listing turned into a deal with tens of thousands of dollars in profit!

Chris Prefontaine: Brian, let's talk about the source first.

Brian O'Neill: The source was an expired listing and they responded via text message to my Slybroadcast voicemail.

Chris Prefontaine: Okay. So, how many attempts? What was the timeframe with the sellers?

Brian O'Neill: They responded to the message relatively quickly, within a day or maybe the next day. Then, our first call was within a couple of a couple of days of that initial exchange.

They had the home on the market, so it was on with an agent. They didn't really have positive feedback there, and I asked him that on the call. Why didn't it sell? Why don't you think it sold? And just the typical stuff that pre-approval buyers will say about the layout or the kitchen or the wall or the paint color or the driveway; the blacktop hadn't been done. Minor stuff that is of concern to us. It wasn't listed for a long time, but they were really trying to maximize their cash out of the house.

Chris Prefontaine: And then, just to put an exclamation point on that for the readers to know, new people always ask, "Well, why don't the buyers care about those things?" It's not that they don't care. They can look beyond those cosmetic issues because you're giving them a pathway to home ownership, right? And some of them thought they couldn't ever get a house. Is that accurate in your opinion?

Brian O'Neill: 100%. Not a single buyer who walked through the house said anything about any of those items I just mentioned.

Chris Prefontaine: Awesome. All right, so let's talk about the deal.

Brian O'Neill: Sure. So again, I asked them the question, what are you hoping to get out of it? If you sold it conventionally, what were you hoping to get out of it? They gave me a range of 60,000 to 70,000 as their goal and I met them in the middle. There was no argument around that. So, their loan balance was $269,752 and they're getting $65,000 on or before the term.

Chris Prefontaine: What were they on the market for?

Brian O'Neill: Their last listing price was $369,000. The asking price was not unreasonable. Again, it was just a matter of, for whatever reason, they couldn't find a buyer conventionally.

Chris Prefontaine: Cool. Alright, so then you structured 36 months, right?

Brian O'Neill: Yes, which initially was not something they wanted to do, but we can discuss that more after we get through the numbers.

Chris Prefontaine: So then, when we went to sell it, you put it on for how much?

Brian O'Neill: $389,900. Again, like I just said, they were on the conventional market for $369,000. My sell price is more than fair.

Chris Prefontaine: Just last night, we were talking with a student about this and he was blown away. He was only going to mark his house up $10,000 and Nick had him going up like $30,000 or $40,000. He was confused on why and how that would work. It's the same logic as the other, right? You lock in your price and they can't wait to have a pathway.

Brian O'Neill: Right.

Chris Prefontaine: Cool. Now, how long did it take you to find this buyer?

Brian O'Neill: It was about 65 days to find this particular buyer. And I went through several.

Chris Prefontaine: Talk about that a little bit. When you say you went through several, what happened?

Brian O'Neill: I probably had a half a dozen next step forms. I had a ton of interest in the house. And I remember when we marketed the property, we marketed multiple areas that exploded with interest because this location is extremely popular right now. So, we had a ton of interest in the home and it took some patience to find the buyer that we ended up selecting.

Chris Prefontaine: You said a few things I want to highlight in case people are new to this type of real estate, because I always assume we're going to roll and people get it. So, first of all, there's an entire module in QLS, our online course, that you can find on our site and it's all about buyers. We're updating these things constantly for the Wicked Smart readers to know. Constantly. This is not a course that gets dust on it. And, so the biggest question we get from the field is, "How do you get them sold?" It's all in there and Brian just follows the system to a tee. Any comments on that, Brian?

Brian O'Neill: Absolutely. You do have to be patient when you're looking for a buyer because you're looking for someone who's going to show themselves. The buyers show themselves when you're matched up with them. And by showing themselves, I mean, they do what you're asking them to do, they follow the steps. When you find that, it becomes an easy decision as long as everything else checks out with the income and the down payment.

Chris Prefontaine: You had a next step form. What did the down payment look like to start? I saw initially it was $12,000 but then you ended at $27,000?

Brian O'Neill: We did. The initial deposit took some finessing. We had some discussions around that because I talked to her about, "Hey, look, it's going to be your deposit plus the first month's rent." And she had a certain number that she just wasn't able to go over day one, which about

$15,000. So, that's why the deposit looks the way it does for signing.

Chris Prefontaine: Again, for anyone new, in a review, you took the first month's rent and you're adding it to Payday #1 because you didn't owe the seller until the following month, correct?

Brian O'Neill: That is correct, yeah.

Chris Prefontaine: Written in our contracts, for you readers, the sandwich lease contracts are going to start 30 days later. If you can negotiate something better, great, but you're going to start 30 days after you install your buyer. So, that first month the buyer pays goes right in your pocket as part of Payday #1. It's all gravy.

So Brian, then when does the other $15,000 come your way?

Brian O'Neill: We're doing three $5,000 payments. I'll get those six months from now, then at the end of 2021, and then in tax season of 2022.

Chris Prefontaine: Got it. So, for Payday #2, this buyer's paying $2,196 a month. What do you owe for a mortgage payment every month?

Brian O'Neill: $1,850. Yeah, a bonus there, the seller has a great mortgage payment. I mean, that's all in for this area. That's low. So, I've been excited about this home since the day I got it because I knew there was going to be a nice spread of about $346 each month.

Chris Prefontaine: Love it. That'll get you just over $12,000 at the end of your term. So, let's talk about Payday #3, if you want to walk them through that.

Brian O'Neill: We had great markup on the home like we discussed. We took it for $335,000 and they were on for $379,000 at one point. So, they took a lot less than they were asking for simply by asking them some questions. This led to a markup of $54,900. The principal paydown on this loan is $450 per month, which comes to $16,200 less the deposit of $27,000 over the course of the term. So, total Payday #3 is $44,100.

DEAL TYPE: Sandwich Lease	DEBT: $ 269,752
SOURCE: Slybroadcast Expired	EQUITY: $ 65,000
TERM: 36 Months	SOLD: $ 389,900

	PAYDAY #1
Deposit from Buyer	$ 12,000 + $2,196 + $15,000 = $29,196
	PAYDAY #2
Monthly Payment	$ 1,850
Payment From Buyer	$ 2,196
Monthly Cash Flow	$ 346 x 36 months = $12,456
	PAYDAY #3
Price Premium	$ 54,900
Principal Paydown	$ 450 x 36 months = $16,200
— Payday #1 Deposit	$ 27,000
Cash Out Payment	$ 44,100

TOTAL PROFIT: $ 85,752

Chris Prefontaine: Which gives you a juicy $85,000 at the end.

Brian O'Neill: Yeah.

Chris Prefontaine: Brian, let's talk a little bit about the seller and then the buyer.

Brian O'Neill: A couple of things on the nuances with the seller was this was not a slam dunk from the initial phone call. You know, a lot of the contracts that I've received have been, they're ready on the first phone call, the motivation's there. So, this was a no, they needed the money to buy the next house or do the next thing that they wanted the equity out of the house. I explained the process to them a little bit more on the initial phone call, sent them the follow-up email, and didn't really have high hopes. Then they messaged me back and said, "Hey, do you have a few minutes to chat?" I had both of them on the phone call, we went through their questions and they said, "Okay, what's the next step?" I said it was to put this in writing.

And you know, I'll come to the house and check it out and if everything checks out, we'll start the marketing – and that's what happened. I went to the house and we had already signed the agreement before I saw the house. So, it wasn't really a sure thing at first, but they warmed up to me and it was just simply following the seven steps to a taken. You know, you've just got to be patient, not everyone is a *yes* immediately.

Chris Prefontaine: You said you signed the agreement before you even went to the house. I'm sure some people are wondering about that.

Brian O'Neill: That's something that's not that challenging to do; at least for me. I sign a lot of agreements before I go see the house and I just make the agreement contingent upon walkthrough of the home. So, if I go to the house and I see something that doesn't look good, you know, I have an out.

But at that point, they were ready. And so, then it was just a matter of putting pen to paper and then me going to check the home. I already had everything lined up, they sent me all the loan information. So, I was good to go.

Chris Prefontaine: So, wait. They send you all the loan information. So, then people say, "Well, how do I ask for that?"

Brian O'Neill: Point #1 is: *Don't make it a big deal.* It's something that is, "I can't help you, Mr. And Mrs. Seller, unless I have that detail." So, if I'm going to the question of what is it that you were hoping to get out of this if you did sell it conventionally with a real estate agent? And then they tell you $60,000 to $70,000, you need to know what the baseline is and that's their balance on their mortgage.

Chris Prefontaine: And, if they're motivated, they'll give it you, right?

Brian O'Neill: Yeah. That and what their payment is. Then I remember asking on the phone, "How much of your monthly payment goes to principal pay down?" And when I say that I just need to verify that when I come to your house, they either show it to me then or they email it to me. But that stuff's easy to get when you don't make it a super big deal. You need that information to be able to provide the solution. You're not trying to probe into their personal life, you know?

Chris Prefontaine: Yeah, I love it. And so, you don't waste a second because you didn't go to the house and kind of dance around. You went to get the thing done unless there was a surprise.

Brian O'Neill: Correct. Yeah. It was just checking a box for me. I already had the agreement executed. I just went to the house to make sure that what I was looking at on the internet and what they were telling me were the same thing.

Chris Prefontaine: So, did I forget to ask you anything about the seller side before we pivot to buyer?

Brian O'Neill: Yeah, the only thing I would say about the seller side was you do have to have open communication with sellers who are living in the house, okay? You know, a vacant house is easy to fill when you find a buyer because there's no one living there. But when they have to find somewhere to go, whether it's buy another house or rent a house and you have a contingency to find a buyer, you have to navigate through that and you have to communicate with both ends as to what the expectations are.

Chris Prefontaine: I love it. Let's talk about the buyer. At the beginning of the chapter, we said, "How do you find the perfect buyer?" So, talk about that a little bit and any nuances that you remember.

Brian O'Neill:	You know, we really did end up with the perfect buyer. And I have buyers in two other houses now that are very similar and it's just uncanny. It's strange how that works out, but not really. So, we had a ton of interest in this house from the day we launched it. And I knew we would because of the area, the location, and the type of house. It's a four bedroom, three bathroom home. I mean, just perfect for a lot of people. So, I probably had six next step forms come in. And, in wanting to do a deal, wanting to get a check, wanting to find a buyer, you have to be patient and understand that all the boxes must be checked; all of them. You cannot let your emotions get in the way of the process. Otherwise, you're setting yourself up for failure with the buyer and, by proxy, the seller.
Chris Prefontaine:	I probably see an area of concern with some of our newer Associates because they're so anxious to get that first buyer. They crammed the wrong person into a house and then, a year later, they have a headache.
Brian O'Neill:	Yeah, which reminds me of one more thing that happened with this particular seller. I was on my last leg, even though I had a few more months to get a buyer, because the sellers were getting tired of all the viewings; there were tons of them. So I said, "Look, we're going to stop the viewings this week if one of these buyers doesn't work out." And it did. But, had it not worked out, this was over. I would've had to give the house back. They were going to stay, they didn't want to move, but this buyer worked out. Like I said, I had gone through five or six previous applicants where

— whether the income wasn't there or the down payment wasn't quite there — they just weren't going through the steps. This buyer did everything the right way.

Chris Prefontaine: You just know. It's like you said, you just know if they're going to be on it.

Brian O'Neill: Absolutely. They show themselves.

SELLING A HOME & EDUCATING THE AMISH //

This Deal Structure Sunday has Chris welcoming Cami & Greg Goucher to discuss how they crafted a deal with a former Amish family, kept an open and honest dialogue with them, educated the couple on how their business works, and then turned a profit. It was quite the experience – one that you're certainly going to want to read more about.

Chris Prefontaine:	Let's go through the basics on this one first and we'll see where it goes. What's the source of this deal?
Greg Goucher:	FSBO.
Chris Prefontaine:	For Sale By Owner. Is there anything time-wise that we should know, like when you called, how long it took?
Greg Goucher:	Actually within 30 days we had this deal signed.
Cami Goucher:	It was quick.
Greg Goucher:	It was real quick.
Chris Prefontaine:	From the call until it was all signed? Just 30 days?
Greg Goucher:	Yes, correct.
Chris Prefontaine:	Nice. It's good for readers to know because I'm always saying with FSBOs, it typically it takes two to four months because of follow-ups, sometimes I've seen them go as long as a year. Okay, and then what was the sale price?

Greg Goucher: $192,500. That's what we tied it up for.

Chris Prefontaine: I'm assuming sandwiched?

Greg Goucher: Yes, sandwiched for 48 months.

Chris Prefontaine: 48, sweet. Again, it's good for the readers to know that these terms are getting longer and longer. You used to primarily see 24-36 month terms, but now we're stretching out to 48-60, some even as long as a decade. This type of deal structuring puts you in a position to be recession resistant. I won't say recession proof, you can't do that, but you can be resistant.

Greg Goucher: Correct.

Chris Prefontaine: So, good job. And then what's the monthly payment on the underlying debt?

Greg Goucher: The monthly payment for them is $1,335.

Chris Prefontaine: $1,335. Is that PITI?

Greg Goucher: It is – Principal, Interest, Taxes, Insurance.

Chris Prefontaine: Sweet. And then, underlying debt. How much do they owe right now?

Greg Goucher: They owe $173, 531.

Chris Prefontaine: So, if they sold to us outright, they weren't getting much, if anything?

Cami Goucher:	They were not, which is why they did it this way with us.
Greg Goucher:	It's why they went with us – because they were angry at the real estate agent. The husband was like, "I don't want to pay an agent that much money."
Chris Prefontaine:	Well, and if they did, by the time they got an offer and then paid the agent, they might come out of pocket even.
Cami Goucher:	They would have. Yeah. That's exactly why they chose to go this route.
Chris Prefontaine:	Alright, so then you only took 30 days, put it on the market through our normal channels, and what happened?
Greg Goucher:	Sure. We put it up for sale for $219,900. We felt like it was a good markup, Cami put it on RentLinx and started marketing the property.
Cami Goucher:	We had to adjust the monthly quite a bit. We followed Nick's aggressive pricing, and we got a lot of kickback on the price because it's out in a rural area. It's not a typical rental, so people, that's their kickback. "I'm not paying that for rent." So, we finally settled on, with everything, $1,561 is going to be the monthly payment.
Chris Prefontaine:	There's nothing wrong with that on a small house.
Cami & Greg Goucher:	No, no.

Greg Goucher:	We had it on the market for 60 days, and we've got over a hundred plus inquiries during the entire time.
Chris Prefontaine:	Wow. And what did you say, roughly 60 days?
Cami Goucher:	Yeah.
Chris Prefontaine:	Okay. So let's go through the numbers. Well, first of all, are there any nuances about the buyer or the seller motivation-wise that we should talk about?
Greg Goucher:	Yeah, well the sellers, they were Amish and they left their sect. And so, they were actually going through quite a learning curve, understanding how this business works and the world right now really. But it was great developing rapport with them. They're a great people, oh my goodness.
	We went to their home and sat down with the sellers and they said, "We're going to do a deal, and we don't care what it's going to take to go ahead and do this deal. We like you guys." And he said, "If you've got to hold onto this thing forever, I don't really care because we trust you guys, because no one else has been really upfront and honest with us."
Cami Goucher:	Yeah. So, down the line it would be good if we could convert this to a Subject To deal, if we had to. I mean, if we got to that point, I think they'd be totally open to that.
Greg Goucher:	They sure would.

Chris Prefontaine: Wow. So, there's two things I'll say and you guys can comment. One is, in about a year, because you got 48 months, in about a year you call the seller and offer them a fraction of their cash-out three years early and you take ownership subject to existing financing? It's possible.

The second thing that came to mind, as you guys just mentioned about truly educating this Amish family, you just affected generations in theory because you just helped them and that's going to change both of your families going forward.

Greg Goucher: Oh, yeah.

Chris Prefontaine: That's pretty cool.

Greg Goucher: Yep, exactly.

Chris Prefontaine: So, let's go through paydays. What's the total Payday #1 upfront and over time?

Greg Goucher: $17,587.

Chris Prefontaine: How much of that was at the signing?

Greg Goucher: $6,597.

Chris Prefontaine: Okay, good. So, that's good for everybody here to know. You got about 1/3 of the down payment upfront. Then the payments are coming when, quarterly, yearly?

Cami Goucher:	It's spread out. They're doing March and October payments. They set it up that way because of tax season.
Greg Goucher:	Right. Plus, the buyer's actually pregnant and due right in the middle of those two payment dates?
Chris Prefontaine:	Nice. So what is Payday #2? Right around $200 a month spread?
Greg Goucher:	Total over time is $4,900.
Cami Goucher:	Yeah. Those numbers are based on a 25-month term that we did with the buyer. So, we actually didn't calculate out the whole 48 months. We're being conservative.
Chris Prefontaine:	Oh, wow. Okay. So, if they do cash out just over 2 years, good for them. If they don't and need to go longer, you don't care. It would be even bigger returns for you at that point.
Cami Goucher:	Correct.
Chris Prefontaine:	And what's Payday #3? When you take the increase in price and principal pay down less the deposit already paid?
Greg Goucher:	$32,026.
Chris Prefontaine:	You look at a spreadsheet, this is how my brain works, and you go, "Okay, we just put another $54,000 into the spreadsheet." I was on a podcast last week and I said

to the host, he's a wholesaler and was blown away by our model, and I said, "You do 12 of these and you've got half a million conservatively, depending on what market you're in. At that point, take six months off, travel, relax, or keep grinding if you want; whatever you want to do."

DEAL TYPE: Sandwich Lease	DEBT: $ 173,531
SOURCE: For Sale By Owner	EQUITY: $ 18,969
TERM: 48 Months	SOLD: $ 219,900

PAYDAY #1	
Deposit from Buyer	$ 6,597 + $10,990 = $17,587

PAYDAY #2	
Monthly Payment	$ 1,335
Payment From Buyer	$ 1,531
Monthly Cash Flow	$ 196 x 25 months = $4,900

PAYDAY #3	
Price Premium	$ 27,400
Principal Paydown	$ 22,213
— Payday #1 Deposit	$ 17,587
Cash Out Payment	$ 32,026

TOTAL PROFIT: $ 54,513

Chris Prefontaine: Pretty cool. $54,513. We talked last night on the Mastermind call, and Zach commented on someone's deal, saying, "That's a whole year's salary." Well, you just did the same thing.

Greg Goucher: Yes. It's terrific. We'll take that any day.

WHAT IF MY DEAL DOESN'T GO FULL-TERM? //

On this Deal Structure Sunday, Chris sits down with Russell Ham from California. As they go over a deal with a 36-month term, Russ vocalizes his concern that the buyers may want to cash out before the end of the deal. How will that impact the home's profitability? Is there still money to be made?

Chris Prefontaine:	So, let's talk about this deal. What was the source?
Russell Ham:	This is expired from a Slybroadcast. I sent out a general voicemail, she called me back and we had a good conversation.
Chris Prefontaine:	The type of deal you structured was which type?
Russell Ham:	It's a 36-month sandwich lease.
Chris Prefontaine:	What do we have for a purchase price? Equity to the seller and the remaining loan balance?
Russell Ham:	The cash to the seller is going to be $415,000 and then the payoff that we agreed on is $420,000.
Chris Prefontaine:	Then you placed a tenant-buyer in that house at what sale price?
Russell Ham:	$860,000.
Chris Prefontaine:	So, not an enormous mark-up. The buyer came in with a down payment initially at what, and then how much over time, just so these guys understand?

Russell Ham:	We got them to 3% up front and then we scheduled four ongoing payments through the term, which will equal $65,000 by the end of the term.
Chris Prefontaine:	Right. In a little bit, I want to go into how the four payments were structured and then why. Over the length of this deal, though, it's a little over $92,000?
Russell Ham:	Yep.
Chris Prefontaine:	That's a nice Payday #1. What about Payday #2?
Russell Ham:	The monthly payment to the seller is $2,531, which is her mortgage and her taxes.
Chris Prefontaine:	Then you got what from the tenant-buyer?
Russell Ham:	$3,200.
Chris Prefontaine:	Almost a $700 spread there.
Russell Ham:	Yep. $669.
Chris Prefontaine:	So Payday #2 is a little over 24 grand. We've got about $116,000 right now, but it's important to know that because he took so much money down upfront and there's not that much of a markup, you'll see what the total profit ended up being. Moving on, what's Payday #3 look like, Russ? We marked the house up from the base of $835,000 to $860,000, leaving a $25,000 surplus.
Russell Ham:	Right.

Chris Prefontaine: Principal paydown is how much per month?

Russell Ham: It's 777. Originally, it was a 15-year loan, which had a huge principal paydown, but she refinanced, but we can talk about that later.

Chris Prefontaine: Yeah, that's super strong. So over time, that's how much?

Russell Ham: Almost $28,000.

Chris Prefontaine: Now, disclosure guys, we're basing these figures on a 36-month term, sometimes a buyer will max this out and push it all the way to the end. Russ's gut on this is they won't. So, we'll give you some other numbers to consider what this deal might look like at a shorter distance. But, sticking with the 36 months, Payday #3 is how much?

Russell Ham: We're in the negative $39,000.

Chris Prefontaine: Because of the big down payment.

Russell Ham: Right.

Chris Prefontaine: So, what Russ is going to do in theory is put a bunch of his down payment aside in order to cover all the money due at cash out. And then if you take all three paydays, Russ, what's your net?

Russell Ham: It's $77,056.

DEAL TYPE:	Sandwich Lease	DEBT: $	420,000
SOURCE:	Slybroadcast Expired	EQUITY: $	415,000
TERM:	36 Months	SOLD: $	860,000

	PAYDAY #1
Deposit from Buyer	$ 27,000 + $65,000 = $92,000
	PAYDAY #2
Monthly Payment	$ 2,531
Payment From Buyer	$ 3,200
Monthly Cash Flow	$ 669 x 36 months = $24,084
	PAYDAY #3
Price Premium	$ 25,000
Principal Paydown	$ 777 x 36 months = $27,972
— Payday #1 Deposit	$ 92,000
Cash Out Payment	-$39,028

TOTAL PROFIT: $ **77,056**

Chris Prefontaine: Your eyes must have gotten a little wide when you saw that big down payment, but there's only so much you can do on a term this short. Even still, this is a phenomenal deal.

Russell Ham: It's an awesome deal. Yeah.

Chris Prefontaine: Alright, so let's dive a little bit deeper into some of the nuances. I have no agenda here, but let's maybe start at the top and say, was there anything about the seller that was worth mentioning, challenging, fun, different, anything at all?

Russell Ham:	I mentioned that originally she had a 15-year mortgage on it, which is a shame that she refinanced because the principal paydown was a little over $2,000.
Chris Prefontaine:	That would have been sweet.
Russell Ham:	But the monthly mortgage payment was really high, so I don't blame her. I would have been worried about that too. But then a month into us talking, she refinanced because she got a really low rate. I looked at it and the principal paydown was still pretty high. I mean, it's over $700. So I still have the benefit of getting a big down payment and now I'm going to get some cashflow out of it as well.
Chris Prefontaine:	Yeah, this is interesting. You could have taken that deal if she never refied. It would have still been okay. What you would have been doing is hammering down principal. So, while there would be a break even on the monthly, you would've made that money up on Payday #3.
	What was the seller's motivation? Because the biggest question I get on podcasts, radio interviews, and live presentations is, "Yeah, but how do you convince a seller?" Which you know we don't, we just solve problems. But what was her deal?
Russell Ham:	So, this is a really cool kind of COVID story. She's a doctor nearby. And so she had it on the market, but she wasn't really liking her real estate agent, which is good for us. Ultimately, she didn't like not being there and having people roaming through her house with

everything going on. So, she just took it off the market. I called her. I said that we could show it in a way that's safe, clean, and with enough notice.

Chris Prefontaine: That's great.

Russell Ham: It was kind of annoying having to set up a viewing instead of just sending a buyer with the code for the lockbox, but it worked out.

Chris Prefontaine: Yeah, and you have the positive energy in this whole thing with how you helped her in a situation that felt very concerning, right? I mean, it's what we do.

Russell Ham: Yeah.

Chris Prefontaine: So, the refi came up. Did it cost her points? I'm just curious, did that cost her a lot of money or did she just roll it all in?

Russell Ham: She rolled it in. I think she owed $305,000-ish, something like that. She took out about $100K, so they rolled it in there and it ended up being that $420,000 balance.

Chris Prefontaine: Which she probably didn't care about because you were taking it over.

Russell Ham: Right.

Chris Prefontaine: For the new people, this is important, you made this deal contingent upon finding your buyer. Obviously, you're not going to take on the weight of a $3,000 payment. That's nice.

You said something earlier about your concern that it won't go the full 36 months. Do you have the math if it only goes 24 months?

Russell Ham: Well, yeah. I should say that we screen each tenant to see how long it will take for them to become mortgage ready. These buyers will probably cash out around the 24-month mark. So, instead of the $77,000, if it goes 24 months, I'll be getting $68,000. Boo-hoo, right?

Chris Prefontaine: I don't think anyone's going to feel sorry for you here, Russ. But that's good for them to know. You're getting that solid cashflow every month. It's all good.

Russell Ham: Right.

Chris Prefontaine: How about the buyer side?

Russell Ham: Yeah, so they wanted to come in just at the 3% mark and we worked with Nick on that. He did obviously a good job of explaining to them that the higher percentage you get, the lender looks at that and says, "Okay, yeah, we're going to get you financed at some point." So, we scheduled incremental deposits throughout the year, higher on the front end and then a little bit lighter on the back end.

Chris Prefontaine: So, it's just a matter of planning out a budget.

Russell Ham:	Yeah. Like, how much can you put down and when can you do it?
Chris Prefontaine:	And what did they do, Russ? I'm just curious why they couldn't qualify today. Most viewers go, "Well, why couldn't they just get a loan?" That's always what I get too.
Russell Ham:	Well, she doesn't work and he's self-employed in construction. Their scores are in the low sixes.
Chris Prefontaine:	So it beat them up?
Russell Ham:	I think there's some seasoning that needs to occur.
Chris Prefontaine:	Some seasoning and maybe some enhancement with credit because the numbers are good.
Russell Ham:	Yep.
Chris Prefontaine:	Okay, really neat. Is there anything else that I didn't ask that the readers might gain a nugget or two from, or did we nail down everything you think?
Russell Ham:	Yeah, I think we nailed it down. Obviously, it's not going to be smooth. Not every deal is going to be smooth. But this one, as far as what I was able to get out of my buyer, it was pretty satisfying as far as the way it went.
Chris Prefontaine:	As one last question, where did you find these buyers? I ask because last night we did a live presentation to a group of investors and, I don't know, with a room of about 32 people, we got asked about eight times,

"Yeah, but how do you find the buyers?" We'd tell them online, Zillow, Craigslist, the usual. "Yeah, but how do you find the buyers?" They just kept thinking it was harder than it was. Do you remember where this buyer came from?

Russell Ham: It was just from our RentLinx inquiry.

Chris Prefontaine: So you answered like we were last night, like, "Yeah, this is just what we do." And they're like, "No, there's got to be something else, like how do you find them?" No, we post where everyone else posts. The difference is, we post seeking what we're looking for, rent-to-own buyer, or you couldn't get financing during COVID, or can't qualify because you're self-employed, whatever. We seek that out in our headlines.

Russell Ham: They're out there. They're out there for sure. When I was going through the process, I was getting five or six calls a day.

Chris Prefontaine: Well, then that's definitely proof that they're out there. Congrats again, Russ.

Russell Ham: Thank you. I appreciate it.

HOW TO HANDLE $25,000 IN ARREARS //

When a homeowner in the middle of a divorce hadn't paid his mortgage in months and couldn't sell the property conventionally, what were his options? Our High 6 Associate Brian O'Neill showed up to handle the situation and give the seller the relief that he needed. What did it cost him? Only $10. This Deal Structure Sunday has Chris and Brian discussing what he was able to pull off and what he ultimately stands to profit.

Chris Prefontaine: First of all, congrats on another deal, Brian. You've been crushing it. To start this one off, can you give the readers a backdrop, like the deal source, why they went with you, a timeline, that whole thing?

Brian O'Neill: Sure, so this was an expired listing, and they went a full six months. The seller was on my list from June until the end of December, just a few days before Christmas. I caught him in early January, as I send out my monthly voicemails, and I think I signed the agreement a week later. I'm fast-forwarding here, but they just didn't really get any traction with the real estate agent. There were some minor inspection items with the house, like some missing carpet in the basement because they had a water issue that was repaired. Then, I came along and was able to provide a solution and really saved the guy money. He was also behind on his payments. He was in forbearance at the time.

Chris Prefontaine: Wow, okay, so there's a bunch of things there. First of all, you didn't talk to him until January? It wasn't like an old expired or an old FSBO, right? You didn't talk to him until the end.

Brian O'Neill: Right.

Chris Prefontaine: Okay, so a bunch of red flags, meaning good things for us, motivation signs, he's behind on payments, frustrated, even though it got fixed. The standard first-time buyer probably got scared off by those repairs. All of these things screamed that they needed your help.

Brian O'Neill: Correct and he wanted to relocate. He wants to relocate from here in Illinois down south to Florida.

Chris Prefontaine: This is kind of a no-brainer really, as far as motivation goes. Let's dive into the actual numbers.

Brian O'Neill: We structured a sandwich lease for 36 months. That was the longest that he was willing to go. He really needed the money – but again, if he would've sold the house conventionally, he would've gotten close to nothing after closing costs and paying his agent's fee. So, we took the house under contract. His loan balance is $280,000 plus the $25,000 that he has in equity. So, that's $305,000, if I can still add.

He was happy with that. That's close to what he was trying to get. He had someone that was making an offer for $295,000 and he was trying to get them up to at least $300K, but the buyer walked away.

Chris Prefontaine: That offer was made while he had an agent, you're saying?

Brian O'Neill:	Right.
Chris Prefontaine:	Yeah, he would've got nothing. Okay, really cool structure and background.
Brian O'Neill:	So, I got him to agree to a 36-month term, which he's a little uneasy with – but at the same time, the multiple motivations are there to be able to wait that length of time.
Chris Prefontaine:	And Brian, I know that you and I do this in our sleep now, but for the readers that don't totally understand it, we don't talk price. We use the sale price of $305,000 for a formula, sure, but we say to the seller, "We're going to get you your loan paid off, and we're going to get you 25 grand at the end," correct?
Brian O'Neill:	Correct, on or before the end of the term. There's no $305,000 anywhere in the sandwich lease agreement.
Chris Prefontaine:	Now, you go to market, let's talk about that. You went on for $359,900, but let's talk about what happened next.
Brian O'Neill:	Sure. We had our list price, but the sale price was actually $356,900. We can talk about the nuances once we get through all of the numbers, but the key thing here is to know that when I first took this house, when I first stepped foot in the house, I knew that I was going to sell it. I just knew it because of the location. It's a four-bedroom house, has plenty of space, and I just knew that I was going to sell this one. I didn't think it

would happen as fast as it did, but I knew it. I told the seller that. I said, "This house is going to go."

We had a few buyers walk through, and the buyer that we ended up selecting really showed herself. And I pretty much think she called me from the driveway after she got out of the house and saw it. So, it was a quick process. She followed all the steps, which is super, super important. She did everything we asked her to do, and we were able to close on this with her very fast.

Chris Prefontaine: Yep, love it. That's how it's supposed to go.

Brian O'Neill: The conversations with the buyer went well and she said she could put $20,000 down initial deposit, which is great. That's about six or seven percent, if my math is correct.

And then when we went through the forms and asked what she would be capable of doing beyond that over the next year or a year and a half, we volleyed back and forth a little bit. Again, we always say, "Hey, this is your plan. You need to be comfortable with it. I'll throw some suggestions out, but ultimately this is your plan." So, she ended up putting down an additional $2,000 per quarter until she got to 10%. And, because it's March, she says, "Well, we'll just do that first quarter payment on the down payment." So, I added another $2,000 to the down and then the first month's rent.

Chris Prefontaine: I love it. So, Payday #1 is that $22,000 plus the first month's rent of about $2,750, putting you at almost

$25,000 with $14,000 more coming. That's a great start.

Brian O'Neill: It is a much easier decision to pick a buyer when they're able to do that.

Chris Prefontaine: Well, and what we didn't say at the beginning of the chapter, but how much did you put down to secure this property?

Brian O'Neill: $10, which I'm going to deliver to the seller on Friday.

Chris Prefontaine: You've got to make it official. We talk about this on podcasts and in workshops all the time, always getting sincere questions like, "Come on, can you really do that?" It's possible. Sorry for the side note and diversion. Let's go to Payday #2.

Brian O'Neill: First off, we're reinstating the monthly mortgage payments. Again, the seller had not been paying them. $2,403 is the mortgage payment, and then we're getting $2,752 from the buyer.

Chris Prefontaine: Wait, so were there any arrears to catch up?

Brian O'Neill: Yes, but it's all getting added to the back of the loan. That's already included into the $25,000.

Chris Prefontaine: And what's your monthly cashflow?

Brian O'Neill: We have a cashflow of $349 per month, which is $12,564 if it goes the full 36 months.

Chris Prefontaine: Yep, sweet. Let's go now to Payday #3.

Brian O'Neill: The markup is $51,900, which is very appropriate based on what he wanted to get for the property. The principal paydown on the loan is $513 a month for a total of $18,468 if it goes full term. Then, we subtract the deposit of 10%. So, we're set for a really nice payday of $34,000 and change.

Chris Prefontaine: Yep, and that gives you a whopping...

Brian O'Neill: 85,684.

DEAL TYPE: Sandwich Lease		DEBT: $ 280,000		
SOURCE: Expired Listing		EQUITY: $ 25,000		
TERM: 36 Months		SOLD: $ 356,900		
PAYDAY #1				
Deposit from Buyer	$ 22,000 + $14,000 + $2,752 = $38,752			
PAYDAY #2				
Monthly Payment	$ 2,403			
Payment From Buyer	$ 2,752			
Monthly Cash Flow	$ 349 x 36 months = $12,564			
PAYDAY #3				
Price Premium	$ 51,900			
Principal Paydown	$ 513 x 36 months = $18,468			
— Payday #1 Deposit	$ 36,000			
Cash Out Payment	$ 34,368			

TOTAL PROFIT: $ 85,684

Chris Prefontaine: And relative to your average, where does this lie out of all your properties? I'm curious.

Brian O'Neill: My average is right about $75,000 for all three paydays.

Chris Prefontaine:	Now, as for the nuances, let's go seller's side first. Just anything and everything so they know that this stuff's real, this is what happens. What happened on the seller's side that you want to share?
Brian O'Neill:	Yeah, this is an interesting one because the seller is an older gentleman, a little bit old school for lack of a better term. And so, we met at his house and then when we put everything in paper and we wrote everything out, and when I actually went to go sign the agreement, I mentioned that we were going to do it via DocuSign. He says, "Well, I don't do that. I don't have a computer." So we actually did it and wrote it by hand. I wrote one up, and then I brought a blank one in case I had to change anything. We're at the house and we're signing everything, and I was actually on the phone with his bank too because I had to make sure that there was a trust thing there as well. He trusted me because I met him in person. We had multiple phone calls, sure, but I just wanted to make certain that we would be able to add the forbearance amounts onto the back of the loan; that he'd be able to do that.
	So we got through that, and then we're going through the agreement. And I said, "Well, is it just you on the deed?" And he said, "No, my ex is on it." I said, "Okay, she needs to sign this."
Chris Prefontaine:	And you were in person getting it signed?
Brian O'Neill:	I'm in person getting it signed, and they're getting divorced. It's not a cordial situation. So he said, "I can call her up." And so he called her up, and she came over.

I waited about 10-15 minutes. She came up and it was watching the two of them go at it while I'm trying to get this thing signed. Thankfully, I had a mask on, so they couldn't see that I was smiling, but I was really kind of having fun with it.

But the point of it is, this was such a chaotic situation. The two of them are going at it. They're bringing me in the middle of it and saying, "I don't mean to bring you in the middle of this, but..." They brought their differences to the table, and I was right in the middle of it.

But, I remember telling my wife later that day, I said, "Because of the fact that I'm prepared for this mentally and that I work on the mental game all the time, I was able to handle it." I never lost my composure. I just kept answering all the questions and eventually we got everything signed. This was the first deal I had done like that where they actually signed in person. So, it was actually comical at the end. It was a little bit difficult going through it, but you get through it, and a deal's a deal.

Chris Prefontaine: Now talk about on their end, I never asked you this, how happy were they when you called and said, "Hey, done deal. We're moving on, done, ready to roll."

Brian O'Neill: He was surprised. He was actually surprised that it happened that fast, even though I told him the first time I met with him that, "This house is going to go. I just know that it is." I'm so confident because I have a buyer profile. I know what people are looking for. Here we had a four-bedroom house with a den, two stories, and a huge yard in a very desirable suburb. I didn't think it would happen that quickly, but I wasn't surprised when it did. And when it happened, now it's real for him and his dream of, "Hey, I get to move. I get to go down south."

Chris Prefontaine: The reason I asked that, Brian, is that we still find people who say, "Well, poor that guy. How could you do that to the poor seller? You took advantage of him." No, no, no, it's quite the opposite. You saved his credit and you saved him. I won't say you saved his marriage because that was already gone, but you got him to Florida and all these good things. It's very healthy.

Brian O'Neill: It is. He gets to go to Florida, which is what he wanted to do, a little bit sooner than he was anticipating. But again, he's not going to complain about that because he couldn't afford this house. So, you're really solving multiple problems because nobody stepped up in the conventional market to try to buy the house; nobody.

Chris Prefontaine: I have a question for you. As good as that deal was at $85,000, do you think in hindsight looking at the numbers, knowing the situation, him getting $25,000 in the end is probably pretty high? Do you think he could've done better?

Brian O'Neill: I do. I could've probably done better on both ends, but again, I'm more than pleased where it is.

Chris Prefontaine: Right, right. There's no reason to get greedy and sloppy.

Brian O'Neill: When I first started off, I think we had one rate adjustment because every three weeks we look at adjustments. And then I gave the buyer a credit because of some of the inspection items; a small one.

Chris Prefontaine: Well, all other things considered, a lesson learned is to check who's on the title, right?

Brian O'Neill: Correct.

Chris Prefontaine: How about on the buyer's side? Any nuances and/or lessons in hindsight?

Brian O'Neill: This is a continuing lesson for me, but it's about the patience it takes on the buyer's side of the business. You have to follow the process and you have to be patient. You have to be willing to walk away from a potential marginal buyer to get to the right one. And I didn't necessarily do that on this house. I didn't walk away from a marginal one, but when she showed herself, she showed herself. It was followed all through the steps, and everything worked out. And I don't know if I could have picked a better buyer. She's one of the best buyers I've had, and did her due diligence as well, which I completely appreciate. So, I know that she'll get to the end.

Chris Prefontaine: Yeah, I love it. And just for the readers to know, that's what we do. Our goal is to get them cashed out. If they screw it all up, whether it's intentional or not, we're not responsible and we can pivot to find another buyer or means of sale. 95% of the time, we're getting to the finish line with our buyers because of the vetting that we do before we place them in a property. That's a pretty cool thing.

Brian O'Neill: I couldn't possibly agree with you more.

HOW MANY PIVOTS CAN YOU COUNT? //

On this Deal Structure Sunday, Chris is joined again by High 6 Associates Greg and Cami Goucher. This deal has all kinds of twists and turns; so many, in fact, that we'd like to see if you can count the number of pivots they made on their way to becoming profitable!

Chris Prefontaine: We're going to have some fun with this one. First, let's talk about the basics, and then we'll get into the weirdness. What's the source of this deal and how did you get it under contract?

Greg Goucher: It's an expired listing... And we got it because it was court ordered. They're selling due to a divorce, so they had to move the property. They'd been trying to sell the home with an agent and actually never even had any showings during the time. The ex-husband was rather frustrated about not getting it sold. We approached him and he loved the fact that we were buying it from him on terms; he'd actually already done terms in the past out in California, so he understood it. He loved the fact that there were no fees, could lock in all the equity, and then be able to split it with his ex-wife.

Chris Prefontaine: How about time from beginning to end? Do you remember anything weird there or just how long did it take?

Greg Goucher: So yeah, we started talking to him at the end of January for my first call. We had our first appointment a couple of weeks later in early February, and then it took us almost four or five weeks to get the taken. It took us some time to work and negotiate it between both ex-husband and wife.

Cami Goucher: But you forgot to say that the ex-wife did not initially agree. Greg had talked to her several times and she would not sign the quit claim deed so we could go ahead and market the property. So, we took a chance and decided to do it anyway. We thought if we brought a buyer to her that maybe she would be more willing. We went ahead and did the contract just with the ex-husband to go ahead and start marketing and see what happens.

We did that and gosh, 40 days into it, we had a buyer we felt really good about. It took probably another seven to ten days to explain to the ex-wife how great of a buyer they were – and we talked them up because they are a great couple. Not that we had to say anything that wasn't true, but we had to get her on board to sign the quit claim deed so we could actually move forward with the deal.

Greg Goucher: Yeah, so we're hung up there for a minute because she wouldn't sign the documents. She wouldn't sign anything. She actually wanted to sell it conventionally because she didn't feel comfortable with the lease purchase.

She was a former real estate agent who had some misconceptions about doing terms, and so it really helped out when we actually got the buyer and I was able to talk to her during those seven to ten days before she agreed. She finally had done some research, looked at the National Property Team and saw that, wow, there's a group of investors with decades of experience doing this. Maybe I don't actually need to be worried.

Chris Prefontaine: So, just to comment on the National Property Team and what that is – if you go to nationalpropertyteam.com, it is really our national group of Associates. We have this website up and it allows a bunch of things – credibility, clearly, that's what happened here, and it allows visitors to see all these different deals and all these different testimonials. You get that when you're an Associate. That was cool you brought that up.

Was there any equity here?

Cami Goucher: $51,079.

Chris Prefontaine: And you got the property under contract for $375,000 – so, they owed just short of $324,000.

Cami Goucher: Yeah.

Chris Prefontaine: Okay. So, what we say for the readers to know is not, "We're buying your home for $375,000." It's actually, "At the end of this 48-month term, we're going to give you your 51 grand equity that you're locking in today and we're going to pay off your loan entirely." It will obviously be a smaller loan 4 years from now, which is how we benefit.

Then you went to the market, as Cami said, for about 40 days-ish and put it on for just under $400,000?

Cami Goucher: $399,900.

Chris Prefontaine: So, the deposit from the buyer was $31,000, which would make your Payday #1 that plus the first month's rent of $2,299. I guess my question is, for the readers to know, where'd the $2,299 come from? Because I see in my notes that they're paying around $2,700 each month.

Cami Goucher: That's just the monthly rent and then he added taxes.

Chris Prefontaine: Okay, so what you did is you didn't take a proration of taxes when you figured their lease for this first month, you just took the regular payment.

Greg Goucher: Correct.

Chris Prefontaine: Okay, you could have gotten away with that. Did you try?

Greg Goucher: We didn't, no.

Chris Prefontaine: It's not that bad. If the figure was bigger, I'd say something. This is PITI, this monthly mortgage payment?

Greg Goucher: Correct.

Chris Prefontaine: Awesome. And so that begs the question that the readers are going, "Well, why direct taxes then?" For marketing reasons only, we sometimes will lower the price to get enough volume on the property. In our videos, it explains to them that we're going to help them understand how to be a homeowner by showing them that you go get a mortgage on the purchase price and then they add taxes afterwards.

Okay, you're making this easy. So, the monthly cashflow is roughly $360 which comes out to... this is all 48 months, right?

Cami Goucher: Yes.

Chris Prefontaine: All right, love it. So, Payday #2 is $17,280. And then to get to Payday #3, we're going to take the surplus, which is $24,900, and we're going to add to it the principal pay down, which is how much?

Cami Goucher: $563.

Chris Prefontaine: That's a great monthly spread. Multiplied by 48 months, that's a paydown of about $27,000, and then we take away the $31,000 that they already gave us up top.

Greg Goucher: Correct.

Chris Prefontaine: So, we have a Payday #3 of roughly $21,000.

Greg Goucher: Correct.

Chris Prefontaine: Alright, cool. Then, if you take all three of these, we're at about $71,000.

DEAL TYPE:	Sandwich Lease	DEBT: $	323,921
SOURCE:	Expired Listing	EQUITY: $	51,079
TERM:	48 Months	SOLD: $	399,900

PAYDAY #1

Deposit from Buyer	$ 31,000 + $2,299 = **$33,299**

PAYDAY #2

Monthly Payment	$ 2,388
Payment From Buyer	$ 2,748
Monthly Cash Flow	$ 360 x 48 months = **$17,280**

PAYDAY #3

Price Premium	$ 24,900
Principal Paydown	$ 563 x 48 months = $27,024
— Payday #1 Deposit	$ 31,000
Cash Out Payment	$ 20,924

TOTAL PROFIT: $ 71,503

Greg Goucher: You got it.

Chris Prefontaine: Did I miss anything in the nuances here in this deal because this took a couple of curveballs. Did we miss any of them?

Cami Goucher: Actually, the closing because this property is two hours away from us. Initially, they had no problems coming up to do the signing with the attorney. The husband works for Coke, they had a surprise audit, and he wasn't able to leave work. So, we pivoted with our attorney asking if it would be okay to do this virtually. The state of Ohio is a little bit lacking with getting the virtual notary, not all the attorneys have it.

Chris Prefontaine: I think everyone in fairness, so many people are going, do we do this or not?

Cami Goucher: And so the buyers were willing to go ahead and go see their own notary. And then I told her she had to overnight these documents to get them back to us by Friday morning so everything could get closed out by the end of the business day. Everything went smoothly until I realized that she didn't send the documents overnight FedEx or UPS, she used USPS priority, so that delayed things a lot. So, that's something new that we will definitely change in the future.

Chris Prefontaine: Well when you think about it all, the readers should know that this is happening right smack in the middle of the first two months of COVID; you two just bobbed and weaved through the obstacles. S

Cami Goucher: Right. It took a little longer than what we would like, but it all closed and everybody was happy. The buyers are ecstatic, the sellers are... The ex-husband is just over the moon.

Chris Prefontaine: You can't get a better win-win-win, energy-wise — especially during a time when, I don't know what they would have done without you guys because they already couldn't sell. How long was that on the market before this?

Cami Goucher: Two years. It had been a long time and, honestly, he told us, "if my ex-wife doesn't sign this so we can sell this property this way, I'm giving it back to the bank. There's nothing else I can do."

Chris Prefontaine:	Okay, so you guys brought up another thing that's worth mentioning. With almost every single Associate that we've sat down with, we teach them about how to become the authority in their market. A big thing that comes out of those discussions is their customer avatar – and that avatar is almost always someone that they care about; someone that they want to help. As a blended family, you guys are into helping blended families or people with family issues. Our whole community is built like that. It's awesome.
Greg Goucher:	Yes, it is. It's awesome.
Chris Prefontaine:	Now, last but not least, I want to bring this up because a lot of people ask us, " Well, what if I'm part time? And what if I want to try this part time?" Can you talk about what you were doing before you joined our Associate coaching program?
Cami Goucher:	I was a nurse practitioner and Greg worked in the trucking insurance industry. Now, we're both full time real estate investors. I made the decision about a year ago to leave my job by this past March – and it happened. Now, not everything's been fabulous and money hasn't been falling from the sky. But, we've done a lot of mindset work, we've had a lot of personal challenges, and I've said this to Greg many times, I feel like our entrepreneurship has really been such a spiritual journey, just testing our faith in ourselves.
Chris Prefontaine:	That's what it does. So, you guys both went from full-time jobs to leaving your jobs and being full-time at real estate?

Greg Goucher: You got it. In 14 months.

Cami Goucher: And we've been loving it.

Chris Prefontaine: And how much profit has there been on your deals in that timeframe? I know it's a rough estimate because payouts can be different as buyers can cash out earlier or later, but roughly?

Greg Goucher: It's about $250,000.

Chris Prefontaine: So, in 14 months, you've made almost a quarter of a million dollars with no previous real estate experience? Bravo.

Greg & Cami Goucher: Thanks, Chris. We appreciate it.

A HOME IN THE MIDDLE OF NOWHERE //

This Deal Structure Sunday is a little bit different. Chris is joined by Chad Heeter to talk about a totally unique property. Though, instead of going over all the numbers up top, they get deep on the nuances of what it's like to try to turn a profit on a home that's completely removed from municipal water, sewer, and power services.

Chris Prefontaine:	What happens when you lose a buyer for a very unique property? I always get asked, "What if you lose a buyer?" And I always say, "There's ways to pivot. Don't worry about it. Just call us, we'll teach you." And some people say, "Oh yeah, yeah, yeah, sure."
	So, Chad had that happen on not just an average, everyday house. I want to talk about the nuances, the lessons he's learned, how he navigated through it. With that as a little backdrop, Chad, why don't you fill us in on the high points?
Chad Heeter:	Sure. I got this property in November of 2019. It was contingent on finding a buyer and that took me five months. And just some background for you because it's an off-grid property that was not finished.
	So it was a new build that they started in 2016. The owner was one of the contractors who I purchased it from. They're a retired couple and they essentially just ran out of steam. I took the property over and it was permitted up to the rough-in plumbing and the rough-in electrical. So, essentially, someone for finishing the

house itself would need to come in and do the flooring or carpeting, sheet rock, appliances, and you'd have a beautiful 2,500 square foot mountainside chalet.

Chris Prefontaine: This is interesting because I also get the question, "What if the house needs work? Do you guys do work?" How much did you spend on the rehab when you first took on this house?

Chad Heeter: I spent zero.

Chris Prefontaine: As long as it's habitable, right? As long as you can get in there.

Chad Heeter: Well, here's the thing. This property came with an RV — a fifth wheel parked right on the property, which is a great incentive for a buyer. And this is what both buyers had done; they live in that RV while they complete the project.

Chris Prefontaine: Just your average everyday property. It's no different.

Chad Heeter: Yeah, so besides that, it's 100% off-grid – meaning that it's solar-powered, has a well for water, and has its own septic system. Buyers would come along and say, "Well, can I connect through electrical?" If you want to invest about $110,000 to draw electricity from a mile and a half away, yeah, you can. All said and done, the home requires a buyer with about $100,000 minimum to finish the property because we then discovered there were some issues with the solar layout as well.

And so, this first buyer that we found last May – a good buyer, passed all the tests, and passed all the screenings. He and his fiancée broke up within the first week of moving in.

When we talk about life events happening with buyers, they're not rare. These things happen all the time. The breakup happened and he thought he could carry on the property, but he couldn't. Not long after, he missed his first payment. At that point, I called you, Chris.

We got on the phone, walked through the whole situation, and I'm saying, "Okay, I've got to pivot, Chris. I've got to pivot, and what do I need to do?" I got an attorney involved in starting the eviction process, sending out the letters. I spoke with Nick along the way as well, who was really helpful in telling me, "You need to send out this letter and you need to keep on him to try to get those payments." In the end, we talked to this guy. We set up a plan for him. We wanted to do right by everyone involved and then he wasn't able to follow through.

Chris Prefontaine: Yeah, I'll chime in there because you made a really good point. We always get on the phone. Even when we say, "I don't know, they're probably just going to give us bullshit," or, "I don't know, I think they're down-and-out," we get on them. We go, "Look, we're here to win. You got in this house to win, you get in this house to cash out, so here's the plan." And we did that for him and he struck out again. You always try morally and ethically.

SMART REAL ESTATE COACH

Chad Heeter:	Sure, sure. You give people the benefit of the doubt until proven that they can't do it. Fortunately, I didn't have to go through a full eviction process. He moved out of the property within two months of his missed payment.
Chris Prefontaine:	Now, like you said, it took you five months to find the first buyer. It was like, "Oh man, I don't know if I want many of these types of properties." Now, of course I'm summarizing Chad, tell me if I'm wrong, but then in the middle of the COVID-19 pandemic, everybody wanted this type of property and you had a bunch of buyers coming out of the woodwork for an unfinished house.
Chad Heeter:	Yeah, so when this went back on the market, basically around January 1, 2021, we were swamped with buyer inquiries because everyone wanted to live on a rural property. It's a beautiful home. For the right person, this is such a great deal. We put it back on the market, but then there was another issue because almost a year had passed. I had it for 36 months, nine months had passed, and we got on the phone with the seller and requested an extension there. Once again, I was reaching out with Chris.

And here's the thing, if you're not leaning on your coach the way that I've leaned on Chris, you don't get it. You're not getting the full benefit of what this Associate program offers at Smart Real Estate Coach. I got on the phone with Chris and say, "I think I'm going to have to have a call with the seller, work out an extension. I don't know how it's going to go." You and I brainstormed |

SMARTREALESTATECOACH.COM   74 those options, got on the call with the seller, and like I feared, they weren't thrilled. But in the end, within a few days, he came around and said, "Okay, well, I'll give you another year."

Chris Prefontaine: Yeah. And I remember on our call, when it was setting expectations that we wanted more time, ultimately we didn't want to argue. He wants a closed deal, this guy, and we do too. But I remember the gentlemen, he had all these things he wanted to talk about it. I just kept telling him, "All we want is an extension. We're trying to win here." And he was okay.

Chad Heeter: Yeah, hats off to you. It's a bit of salesmanship to keep him grounded in terms of like, "Okay, what do we ultimately want? We want to get cashed out and you want to get cashed out. And, if we have a little more time, it's still going to be a win-win."

Chris Prefontaine: In the end, after we got off the call, I remember you and I saying, "Look, if he doesn't give us the extension, we're okay, but it would be really cool to get an extension." We're making monthly principal-only payments, which we'll talk about in just a minute. This is a sweet deal.

Chad Heeter: Yep.

Chris Prefontaine: Okay, so fast-forward, Chad. You had a whole bunch of new inquiries, but this final buyer was a serious buyer who came from far away, did inspections and everything.

Chad Heeter: He's definitely a serious buyer. I had gone through so many buyers visiting the property. In the end, it's a property at 9,000 feet, you've got to live off-grid, and you've got to finish the property. So, you've got to have $100k+ of funds that you can verify right off the bat.

I would be talking to people and I'd say that within the first couple of lines. "Hey, I know you're interested in the property. Do you have $100,000 that you can verify to go forward?" And I only took a couple serious buyers at that point. This guy, he was a contractor. He lived in Las Vegas. They loved the property, as we discussed. They came out. He and his son and his wife drove out one weekend, which is I think an eight-hour drive, and spent two or three hours with me around the property, which is unusual too.

I wouldn't normally spend that much time with someone, but he was going over the property with a fine-tooth comb. He ended up coming back two weeks later and doing it again. After that first meeting, I thought I had him locked up, but he called back three days later and said, "The numbers just aren't working." So, I thought I lost him. Then he ended up calling back maybe a week later and said, "You know what? I've got an offer for you."

Chris Prefontaine: Because you got all the inspections and all the potential headaches over with up front, he brought a cashier's check, signed off, and it was a done deal. I'm sure you would love to find 10 buyers like that, right?

Chad Heeter: Exactly.

Chris Prefontaine: All right, so let's talk about some serious numbers here. What do we have going on here?

Chad Heeter: This was an owner-financed deal. It was an expired listing that I got through Slybroadcast. The sellers are a retired couple and they just ran out of steam to complete this house. I got it for $431,000 for 36 months, and with an extension it became a 48 month term.

Chris Prefontaine: What was the sale price?

Chad Heeter: $460,000.

Chris Prefontaine: Now, just for the readers, remember that he sold this home to the second buyer at the same price he did the first buyer. This means that he had already paid down the principal a bit, which you're going to see here in a minute.

Chad Heeter: Yeah, so with this new buyer, Payday #1 is $20,000.

Chris Prefontaine: So, last Saturday you collected $20,000 plus the first month's payment?

Chad Heeter: Correct. Yeah, so unique to this deal... I don't always offer credits, but when you listen to the breakdown of why this was a special property, this buyer gave us two options, one at full price at $460,000 with a $400 monthly credit, or take it with no credit at $440,000. And the reason we went ahead and did the credit was because he's a contractor. He's probably going to cash out early, meaning that he's probably not going full term. That's his intention and that's my bet as well, that this'll probably be wrapped up within 18 months. Meaning that 18 months at $400 credit is $7,200, which is less than that $20,000 price difference that he was looking for if I didn't take the credit.

Chris Prefontaine: And not only that, but let me add this – the likelihood of this gentleman putting that kind of money in, doing that kind of due diligence, and defaulting is probably next to nil.

Chad Heeter: Right.

Chris Prefontaine: But when we looked at the offers, if there was a default, Chad would have still gotten more cash flow and more protection for himself, right? So it's a win-win all around.

Chad Heeter: Sure.

Chris Prefontaine: And every month he's getting $1,200 off principal. Go ahead, Chad.

Chad Heeter: Payday #2, at this point it's zero because his payment with the credit negates any monthly spread.

So, Payday #3, on the back end, there's a $29,000 surplus, the difference between that $431,000 and $460,000. Principal pay down, again, that's principal paid on the 36 months for this new buyer if he went the full 36 months, so that's not including the 12 months that I've already had.

Chris Prefontaine: There's actually an additional 12 months times $1,200?

Chad Heeter: Well, we won't go into all the weeds, but my buyer stopped paying six months in.

Chris Prefontaine: Okay, so an extra $6,000. It's not much to write home about, but it gave you a buffer to turn the property.

Chad Heeter: And the point is, I'm basically at even, because that first buyer put down $15,000. Out of that money, $8,000 went to covering closing costs because this is an owner-financed deal. Then, essentially, there's the remainder that I kept in the bank, which went towards paying down the months that he did not pay.

Chris Prefontaine: But, that brings up something. You've got $1,600 a month coming in. Technically, there is a $400 spread, but with the way you structured the credit you have to give this gentleman at the end, you're technically socking away that money just in case. If he ever defaulted, you're fine, but you're technically socking it away.

Chad Heeter: Correct.

Chris Prefontaine: Got it. Okay, so then we subtract the deposit you got and we're left out with about $70,000 plus any peanuts left over from the calculation you just did.

Chad Heeter: Yeah, so if it goes full term... I don't think it's going to go full term, so this may be more like a $45,000 deal.

Chris Prefontaine: This is probably the smallest deal you've done on owner financing, right?

Chad Heeter: Yes, this is a small deal. The others I did were over $100,000. But, at the end of the day, worst case scenario I'm still walking away with mid-5 figures.

DEAL TYPE: Owner Financing	DEBT: $ 0
SOURCE: Slybroadcast Expired	EQUITY: $ 431,000
TERM: 48 Months	SOLD: $ 460,000

PAYDAY #1	
Deposit from Buyer	$ 20,000 + $1,600 = $21,600
PAYDAY #2	
Monthly Payment	$ 1,200
Payment From Buyer	$ 1,600 ($400 Credit)
Monthly Cash Flow	$ 0
PAYDAY #3	
Price Premium	$ 29,000
Principal Paydown	$ 1,200 x 36 months = $43,200
— Payday #1 Deposit	$ 20,000
Cash Out Payment	$ 52,200

TOTAL PROFIT: $ 73,800

Chris Prefontaine: Anything else we missed that you want to share?

Chad Heeter: Just, don't sweat it too much. Sure, it could be a little nerve-wracking at times, and this had its moments for me. But I was so grateful to have Chris to call up and say, "Hey, am I thinking this through correctly, and what's the next step?"

Chris Prefontaine: So, we'll let you cry on my shoulder with the $45,000 to $70,000 profit potential here. All kidding aside, you did an awesome job, Chad.

HOW TO STRUCTURE A 10-YEAR TERM //

On this Deal Structure Sunday, Zachary Beach sits down with Certified Coach Mike Makredes and our Associate Russell Ham. With this deal, the sellers wanted the house sold in a matter of months, but Russell and our team were able to talk them into a 10-year term. How did they pull that off?

Zachary Beach:	So Russell, what some people might not know about you is that it took you roughly 12 months in order to get your first deal under contract. Obviously, you're in a tough market, but do you feel as though your return on investment is worth it?
Russell Ham:	Of course, because there was no money out of my pocket.
Zachary Beach:	No, absolutely. I just want, for those who are out there to know, Russell comes from a background with zero real estate experience; he's a teacher. It took him maybe a little longer than most during this time, but he has shown some amazing resilience, some grit, and now has a fantastic deal.
	So, with that as a backdrop, let's start on this deal. Can you hit me with maybe a little background on this deal between you and Mike? Tell me where you found the sellers and maybe some of the nuances about the deal before we dive into the actual numbers.
Russell Ham:	Yeah. This was an expired listing and they were super interested in what we had to offer. So, I went on an appointment and the first thing they said as soon as I

got there was, "This might not be a good deal for you, because we need to sell by April in order to avoid capital gains." We sat in the kitchen and I called Mike, so we had a little conference call. Mike was able to discuss with them the possibility of going a little bit longer and using this as their investment, maybe even gear it towards their retirement. They're teachers out in the Palm Springs area, so they're looking forward to retirement.

Zachary Beach: Okay. Mike, how'd that conversation go? Because obviously you go from, "Hey, we're going to need to sell this thing or we're going to be hit with capital gains," to, "alright, now it's going to be a 10-year deal." How'd that conversation go, Mike, and how'd you make that pivot?

Mike Makredes: Well, I knew that we had a short amount of time even if we were going to sell traditionally; especially for full market price. Normally if you want to sell something fast, you have to discount the price just to move it quickly. So, I was thinking, "Okay, if you're going to take a hit on this with capital gains, let's see how we could recapture that through the payment," because I knew that their mortgage payment was really low compared to the rents in the area. And so there is a spread there where they could make some money over time to offset those capital gains and actually make a lot more and still get full market value on the property.

Selling on our terms, they're going to come out way ahead. I knew they had time on their side and they weren't in a hurry to get that money. They didn't need the money. The house was vacant. So, as long as we could guarantee they wouldn't lose out on the tax situation, it was actually pretty easy to put together.

So, we did our research and we can go back to the initial conversation. It was a long conversation. They had quite a few questions in the kitchen there, but we had them on speaker phone with Russell there, and we basically just went over all their concerns. "How can we profit off of this? How long of a term are you looking to do? Do you need the money right now to take out the equity and use it towards something?" It was just a matter of making them comfortable with us and building a little bit of a rapport, because in the terms business, what we do is not the norm. People aren't used to it. So, it takes a little bit of educating, and we did that and made them feel really comfortable.

Zachary Beach:	Awesome. I appreciate a little bit of background there. So, let's start from the top here. What type of deal is this?
Mike Makredes:	It's a lease purchase.
Zachary Beach:	Okay. And the source was?
Mike Makredes:	Expired.
Zachary Beach:	Perfect. Okay. Purchase price?
Mike Makredes:	$865,000.

Russell Ham:	There's $605,000 in equity and the balance of the loan is $260,000.
Zachary Beach:	Okay, cool. And the term is 10 years?
Russell Ham:	Yes.
Zachary Beach:	Alright. So, for the readers to know, we haven't sold this property just yet, but what we're going to do is we're going to go over some projections on this property, and we'll actually go over all of the projected profits or three paydays for the 10 years.
Zachary Beach:	So, sell price. What is your projected sell price on this?
Russell Ham:	$890,000.
Zachary Beach:	And that's what the comps are telling us in the area. Roughly $890,000 today if you sold it conventionally?
Mike Makredes:	Yeah, there's a range, but we're in that price range in that community, yeah. It's around there. You could definitely get that.
Zachary Beach:	Okay. Let's talk about the projected Payday #1, which is your non-refundable deposit that you're going to collect from your buyer.
Russell Ham:	So, if we do 10%, then we're going to be collecting 89,000.
Zachary Beach:	So just in case you're out there wondering how an almost 6-figure down payment is possible – it's 10% of an almost $900,000 house, which is definitely

reasonable. Our down payments typically fall between 6% and 10%. In my opinion, selling a $900,000 house without at least a plan to get them up and over 10%, I wouldn't be very excited to place a buyer in this property without at least getting that amount.

Before we go further, I know there's a few nuances here, because your sellers were a little difficult.

Mike Makredes: Well, it's not that they were difficult. It's just taken us about 90 days to get to the point where the home is actually under contract with us. They ended up going with a real estate agent just to see if they could sell it before that April capital gains deadline. Unfortunately, they didn't go with us first, even though we had a better plan. They really wanted to try and get it sold on their own. So, we backed off and we let them do that. Of course, they have the right; it's their home.

We did keep in contact, though. Russell was checking in every so often. I would say maybe every three, four, or five weeks, right, in between just to let them know that we're still there. And they ended up not being able to sell. They didn't even get an offer. Like I said, to sell it that fast, they would have probably had to discount the property. So, they didn't get the price they wanted, and they ended up firing the agent, and they came back to us.

Zachary Beach: A majority of our deals are actually going to take 90 - 180 days to get the seller fully under contract, because there's multiple options out there. They were trying to sell this house as quickly as possible to eliminate the capital gains. Then what they needed to do was pivot, obviously, since they weren't able to sell in that fast a period of time. So, it's a fantastic deal for you guys to step back into.

Tell me about the monthly payment, because there's a couple of things happening here with the monthly payment. So, what is the actual payment that the seller has with PITI?

Russell Ham: $2,300.

Mike Makredes: That's including HOAs, the solar payment that they have and, of course, taxes and insurance. They were renting the property for $3,800 though, so we kew that we had some room to play.

Zachary Beach: So, you guys decided to do what? Give them additional money each month in order to satisfy them?

Mike Makredes: Yeah. They wanted to look at it as an investment since they know they can make $1,500 in spread. They wanted to still keep that if they were going to go on a long-term lease. So, we're going to take it to market at $4,100. We feel like we can get that, just because it has a solar now, so they get their money and we're going to make a $300 spread.

Russell Ham: We'll take it to market and if we need to drop it a little bit to be more competitive, we definitely have the room to do so. They want to try to maximize this investment, so we'll see what we can do for them.

Zachary Beach: It's over-the-top important here to know that when you took the property under contract, you negotiated the best you could when it came to the actual terms of the agreement. And then we're going to take it to market and we're going to see if there needs to be any adjustment. You can always renegotiate.

Mike Makredes: Right.

Zachary Beach: So your potential from your buyer is you're thinking $4,100 per month?

Russell Ham: Yep. With a monthly cash flow of roughly $300.

Zachary Beach: Do you know how much is taxes? Because if you use some of our techniques, you can certainly add the taxes back in, as our buyers do pay the taxes. Or what we do is we set them up so they understand that this is how much they would pay in taxes, and that would be part of their monthly payment. We can prepare them for once they go get their own loan. So, you could potentially create a additional spread for that. That's more than likely going to come into play in your marketing when you're dealing with higher numbers here.

Mike Makredes: Absolutely.

Zachary Beach: Now, for Payday #3, we've got a surplus on the home's sale of $25,000. What's the principal paydown?

Russell Ham: $570, which is $68,400 if it goes full term.

Zachary Beach:	Obviously that's a huge piece. Adding the surplus onto that and then subtracting the original payday, which is $89,000, you're left with about $4,400.
Mike Makredes:	Right.
Zachary Beach:	So, you're getting your majority of money up front, which is 100% okay. You get this person invested in the property on a long-term deal, because obviously a huge piece of the deal is your principal pay down and your spread. In the end, what kind of profit are you looking at on this deal?
Mike Makredes:	Including the first month's rent, it's $133,500.
Russell Ham:	Not too shabby.

DEAL TYPE: Sandwich Lease	DEBT: $ 260,000
SOURCE: Expired Listing	EQUITY: $ 605,000
TERM: 10 Years / 120 Months	SOLD: $ 890,000

	PAYDAY #1
Deposit from Buyer	$ 89,000 + $4,100 = **$93,100**
	PAYDAY #2
Monthly Payment	$ 2,300
Payment From Buyer	$ 4,100 ($1,500 Credit to Seller)
Monthly Cash Flow	$ 300 x 120 months = **$36,000**
	PAYDAY #3
Price Premium	$ 25,000
Principal Paydown	$ 570 x 120 months = $68,400
— Payday #1 Deposit	$ 89,000
Cash Out Payment	$ 4,400

TOTAL PROFIT: $ **133,500**

Zachary Beach: Awesome. As you can tell, Russell is a very humble man – and now he's $133,500 richer. So congrats to you, Russell, on this deal. And congrats to you, Mike, on coaching him through it. It's another fantastic deal for the Wicked Smart community. Do you guys have any parting words for the community before we hop off?

Mike Makredes: I just wanted to say that you should stay the course, stay committed, and stay consistent with your work. You will be rewarded for it. None of it goes to waste. A perfect example is Russell here. It took him a while to get his feet off the ground, but that tree is now bearing fruit. He's got a few other deals that are in the pipeline that should be going through. I told him earlier that the floodgates are going to start opening. Once you get that first deal, everything starts to click. It's funny how it works. So congrats, Russell, again. It's a great, great deal he put together there.

Russell Ham: Thank you. I appreciate your help, too.

HOW TO MASTER CREATIVE REAL ESTATE //

THE FIRST STEP TOWARDS MAKING 3 PAYDAYS™ PER DEAL

With QLS, the goal is to get you everything you to need to do 5-6 figure deals on your terms. Whether you want to supplement your income or you want to replace your income, it doesn't matter (think about what one deal alone can do for you this year, never mind one per month eventually).

Within a few weeks of studying the QLS, we'll have you generating approximately 6-10 leads weekly. But, is this an overnight way to get rich? Unlike most educators, we'll tell you NO. Most of our students do their first deal in 90-180 days — and some take longer.

But, quite frankly, who cares if you take 6 months or 9-10 months to get rolling when you know you're going to be averaging $75,000 per deal potentially. On the high end, we've helped students make as much as $250,000 (and if you're on the lower end of our averages around North America, would you be okay with $45,000 on a deal?).

Once you get this down, you will have this ability for life. And if you want to make more, our team can help you plan out your goals and show you how to use the QLS Home Study Program to reach it predictably.

With QLS, Here Are All The Benefits You Get

With QLS, you're going to discover...

- How to **create 3 Paydays™ per deal** instead of feeling like you're on a treadmill, creating one paycheck per deal, and having to do it all over again.
- How to get **potential buyers and sellers emailing, calling, and texting you every month** to do deals with them – at little to no cost.
- Our secrets to **getting the BIGGEST monthly payments and upfront payment from your buyers** – this way you pocket more up front and create PASSIVE income.
- How to set up the perfect terms, so you are always creating a win/win/win.
- The easy **step-by-step road map you can follow to quit the rat race** in 12-24 months or less and keep your real estate deals for supplemental income.
- How to get trained virtual assistants and a fully automated phone-dialing system that do almost all of your calling AND will save you from cold-calling yourself. *We only want you speaking with sellers that WANT to speak with you.*
- How to give yourself **5-figure "surprise paydays"** in February and March as buyers get their tax refund – and make enough so you can take the rest of the year off (if you want to, that is).
- The **exact legal, tax, and insurance documents** that our attorneys have spent 500+ hours putting together — all assembled in ready-to-use templates.

- The **"rejection-proof" scripts** you repeat every time you want to close a deal.
- How to get a financial commitment from a buyer without taking your house off the market.
- How to do deals in your IRA or Coverdell.
- And much, much more!

Plus, There's A Money-Back Guarantee!

With our 30-Day Money-Back Guarantee, there is absolutely NO RISK — we just removed it for you. But, to make you feel at ease, here's our **unconditional guarantee**:

You have 30 days to return QLS for a 100% refund, if for any reason you don't feel it's for you. No reason needed, no questions asked. So, again, there is Absolutely No Risk — we just removed it for you!

How Do I Get Started?

Simply visit **www.GetQLS.com** and select which plan works best for you. It's that easy!

EPILOGUE //

What comes to mind for me as we wrap up this book is the importance of association and the importance of who you hang out with – your peer group. We are super conscious of this and, as such, constantly expose our community to infinite ways of collaborating with the best minds out there.

Every single day, our Wicked Smart Community of 90 Day Jump Start and Associate members are on Slack together. If this Slack community was all we offered, it would be worth the entire investment of those levels. In Slack, you're surrounded by over one hundred like-minded individuals from all different backgrounds. When you ask a question, everyone cannot wait to dive in and help. Just as I'm writing the epilogue and finishing up this book on a Sunday morning, I see a question that was posted and members of the community are lining up with advice before I had a chance to chime in. So, you can see first-hand what I'm referring to here before actually becoming a part of this amazing community.

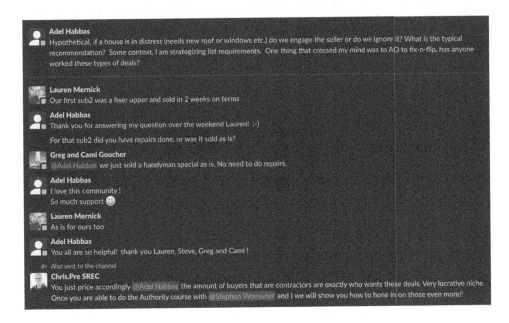

In addition to Slack, we gather weekly on a private video call for Associates Only. These sessions add additional value, skills, systems, and mindset – as well as unlimited Q&A and support from and for each other. On top of all of this, we also come together for a full day prior to our two (of four) major events in April and September for an Associate Development Day.

Outside of the Wicked Smart Community, we realize that, as Dave Ramsey stated, *"Thoroughbreds don't run with donkeys."* On a weekly basis, I'm hanging out, speaking, and interviewing with some amazing investors, thought leaders, and sought-after professionals. As I do that, we bring those people to the Wicked Smart Community because we know that your peer group determines literally everything relative to your future. Specifically, learning from those that have gone through the growth stages of a small business, experienced hardships, and have flat out "been there before," will allow you to develop a well-rounded Genius Model that enables you to crank out 3 Paydays™ how and when you'd like to.

I urge you to plug into our weekly interviews on the Smart Real Estate Coach Podcast to hear from guests that will always leave you walking away with a major nugget or two. Come rub elbows in the Wicked Smart Community with the best of the best.

ABOUT THE FAMILY //

At *Smart Real Estate Coach,* **we empower individuals and families to create the life of their dreams**. *We encourage aspiring investors and entrepreneurs to take the first step towards creating REAL income with real estate.*

CHRIS PREFONTAINE
Founder & CEO

Chris Prefontaine is a 3-time best-selling author of *Real Estate on Your Terms*, *The New Rules of Real Estate Investing*, and Moneeka Sawyer's *Real Estate Investing for Women*. He's also the Founder and CEO of SmartRealEstateCoach.com and host of the Smart Real Estate Coach Podcast.

Chris has been in real estate for almost 30 years. His experience ranges from constructing new homes in the '90s and owning a Realty Executive Franchise to running his own investments (commercial & residential) and coaching clients throughout North America.

Today, Chris runs his own buying and selling businesses with his family team, which purchases 2-5 properties monthly, so they're in the trenches every single week. They also help their Associates and students do the exact same thing all across North America.

Having been through several real estate cycles, Chris understands the challenges of this business and helps students navigate the constantly changing real estate waters.

ZACHARY BEACH
Partner & COO

Zachary is an Amazon best-selling author of *The New Rules of Real Estate Investing* and co-host of the Smart Real Estate Coach Podcast. He is a Partner, COO, and Coach at Smart Real Estate Coach. In September 2020, they released a revised edition of *Real Estate On Your Terms*, which Zach co-authored.

At the age of 25, Zach decided to leave the world of bartending and personally training and jump into the family business. It was one of the first big risks that he took in his life, as nothing was guaranteed. Plus, he knew absolutely nothing about real estate. Through hard work, in-house training, and implementation, Zach has now completed over 100 deals and growing. On top of that, he coaches students around the country on how to buy and sell property just like his family still does. Now, as a group, they buy and sell 20-30 properties a month with a predictable and scalable system, controlling between $60 million+ of real estate at any one time with little to no money in the deal and no banks involved.

Zach has been in the business for over 4 years and now runs all operations of Smart Real Estate Coach, on top continuing to coach his students and Associates. He has an amazing wife Kayla and two small children, his son Remi and his daughter Bellamy. He is a prime example of how to be successful both in business and at home.

NICK PREFONTAINE
Partner & Coach

In 2003, Nick was in a snowboarding accident that left him in a coma for over 3 weeks. The doctors told his parents that he probably wouldn't walk, talk, or eat on his own again. Less than 3 months later, he was running out of Franciscan Children's hospital. Now a Certified Infinite Possibilities Trainer, Nick speaks to groups that benefit from his message of overcoming adversity.

Nick grew up in the real estate industry and got started on his own at an early age. Most notably, he was knocking on Pre-Foreclosure doors at 16, doing up to 50 doors a day. This helped shape Nick's career.

Now, Nick specializes in working with lease purchasers to get them into a home and on the path to home ownership. Regardless of a buyer's credit situation, he looks at their complete financial picture and comes up with a plan to get them into a home.

ABOUT THE HIGH 6 ASSOCIATES //

These aren't fly-by-night landlords or novices in this business. All together, they're part of a large, national network of Rent-To-Own real estate investors.

BRIAN O'NEILL

Brian and Katie O'Neill are real estate investors and business owners. They have been happily married for 10 years and enjoy spending time with their son, Will.

BKW Property Solutions was started to provide flexible real estate solutions for both buyers and sellers. They serve the Greater Chicagoland area and help buyers realize their dream of owning a home. When Brian and Katie experienced many of the common challenges of selling their own home many years ago, they knew there had to be a better way. That is the foundation of BKW Property Solutions and we look forward to serving your needs. There is a better way!

RUSSELL HAM

Our passion is to find home buying, renting, and selling solutions for every person that we work with. We're a small family-owned business working in the Riverside, Orange, and San Diego County, CA area that specializes in Lease Purchase / Rent-To-Own options for both buyers and sellers.

Our team has been around the real estate business for many years and focuses on purchasing homes via Lease Purchase, Owner Financing, and other non-conventional methods. We assist buyers with a plan to gain the time they need for credit repair, mortgage qualifying, seasoning, or building up a down payment.

We help families accomplish their dream of home ownership as well as partner with sellers that receive full market value for their homes. We usually buy between 3-5 properties monthly and a large percentage of those are done with creative financing.

Since we started our company, we've treated every customer and team member like they were a part of the family. We know that there are other companies out there who offer similar services, but we take great pride in our commitment to helping people — and that commitment also comes with a personal touch that has given us our reputation for integrity and excellence. We feel confident you'll enjoy working with us!

CAMI & GREG GOUCHER

Greg and Cami are happily married with a blended family of five kids. We live in Northeastern Ohio and love to travel. We understand the challenges and complexities of life, including: divorce, job loss, legal battles, not to mention buying and selling a home.

If you're looking for a solution to your real estate issues, we are here to help you. Our team is flexible, very easy to work with, and has a proven track record of making win-win deals for both the seller and buyer.

If you are looking to sell, We pay full market value through various lease purchase options that benefit all parties involved. We work with you to see which option is the best fit for your situation.

If you're looking to buy, but can't qualify for a traditional mortgage due to credit issues for whatever reason, this could be just what you need to obtain the American dream of owning your own home. We can help you.

CHAD HEETER

With over 20 years of real estate experience, we're building a family-run real estate investment company based in beautiful Salida, Colorado.

Chad Heeter grew up in a Kansas City real estate family. At 7 years old, he was pulling weeds and picking up trash around the 30+ rental properties that his dad owned. Soon, he was promoted to mowing lawns and painting. Years later, Chad continued on his own, purchasing and rehabbing his own rental properties. After his wife, Elizabeth, passed away in 2017 after 16 years of marriage, Chad needed to focus on raising his children on his own. He decided to get back into real estate investing, something he could manage while the kids were in school.

Not long after, Chad was introduced to Chris Prefontaine and National Property Team. He's proud to be connected to this incredible group of investors who are working to build win/win relationships by solving problems that many home sellers face, as well as helping home buyers achieve their dream of owning a home.

Our passion is to find home buying and selling solutions for every person that we work with. Buffalo Peak Property Solutions is a locally-owned & operated real estate investment company and we work throughout Colorado.

Since we started our company, we've treated every customer and team member like they were a part of our family. We know that there are other companies out there that offer similar services, but we can proudly say that we take great pride in our commitment to helping people, and that commitment also comes with a personal touch that has given us our reputation for excellence. We know you'll enjoy working with us, whether you're selling your house or wanting to become homeowners!

WHY JOIN THE WICKED SMART COMMUNITY? //

We seek results and create deal-makers. With a community of students and Associates spread across North America, we think that instead of taking it from us, you should listen to them. These are real clients with real results.

"Being an Associate has been life changing. I'm surrounded by a family who is committed to helping me succeed and I'm being empowered to grow and transform my life, my business, my finances, and my community in the process!"
– Monica Scott / California

"Being an Associate means being with a like-minded community of successful entrepreneurs who want to make a huge positive impact in people's lives. We love growing with alongside them. Where else can you get to live a life like this and be handed a blueprint -- not only in the terms business, but in life."
– Greg & Cami Goucher / Ohio

"Being an Associate in this community has changed my entire life. This group is special. We all have a common goal, and we lift each other up. There is limited to zero negativity and we don't use the words "can't" or "won't". I've never been a part of anything like this and I'm eternally grateful."
– Brian O'Neill / Illinois

"Being an associate means being part of a family. Chris, Zach, Nick, and the rest of the SREC team have allowed me to grow and learn a niche in real estate I never thought possible. I'm forever grateful for making the decision to join knowing that this family will be with me every step of the way."
– Russell Ham / California

"Being an associate means being part of a family of consistently supportive, helpful, and kind people. Joining this community has been life-changing for us. We've been able to move toward the life we wanted for us and our kids, while

meeting awesome people along the way. We made the decision to apply to SREC and haven't looked back since."
– Lauren Mernick / Connecticut

"I can't tell you how happy I am with my decision to join your team. Smart Real Estate Coach is an outstanding business that will continue to grow and thrive -- and I'm delighted to be part of it. You inspire me to greatness and I promise I won't let you down."
– Bill Reich / Washington, D.C.

"Over the past 3.5 years, while working through tons of personal turmoil, the one thing that has remained constant has been this community. I'm deeply appreciative of the people and the support I find within the group that have led to 20+ takens and approaching 20 solds. For those of you wondering about the magic that has gotten me that many deals, here it is: ACTIVITY. Nothing more. Nothing less." **– Link Ervin / North Carolina**

"Being an associate is an opportunity not only to stand on the shoulders of giants, but also to have a seat at their dinner table."
– Robert Purcell / Michigan

---

products that we believe will help your business, we do not recommend investing into anything without doing you own due diligence. Like with anything in life, in order to succeed, you will need to put forth effort and be persistent. And finally, any information provided is education and cannot be taken as legal or financial advice.

We are not attorneys. Laws change in every State from time to time. Always check with your attorney before buying and/or selling real estate for the applicable laws in your area. These laws may or may not affect some of the techniques we teach. There are no laws to our knowledge that can STOP you from profiting in real estate, but you'll need to seek a qualified local real estate attorney.

As of the posting of this disclosure, we are aware of laws in the following areas that are different from the other States. This is not all inclusive and only those that we are aware of:

- Texas: Lease/purchase restrictions unless you comply with local changes.
- Maryland: Foreclosure laws within 20 days of foreclosure. We don't teach foreclosure. Some restrictions buying subject to existing mortgages.
- North Carolina: Comply with 3-day right of rescission as well as recording agreements when doing lease/purchase.
- California: Foreclosure property laws. We don't teach foreclosure.
- Florida: Licensing laws for lease purchase if you have a Seller Specialist working for you acquiring properties.
- Illinois: Assignment restrictions for wholesaling and AO deals.

Made in the USA
Monee, IL
17 February 2022

91384492R00066